Russell Punter

Illustrated by David Semple

Bruce and Sue are at the docks.
They're going on a cruise.

Their nephew Lou is coming too.

This way please, cockatoos!

"Woo-hoo!" shouts Lou,
who's only two.

"Stay by my side," says Sue.

They reach their cabin.

What a view!

Bruce turns around.

Where's Lou?

They head on deck.

He can't be far.

A cry comes from the pool.

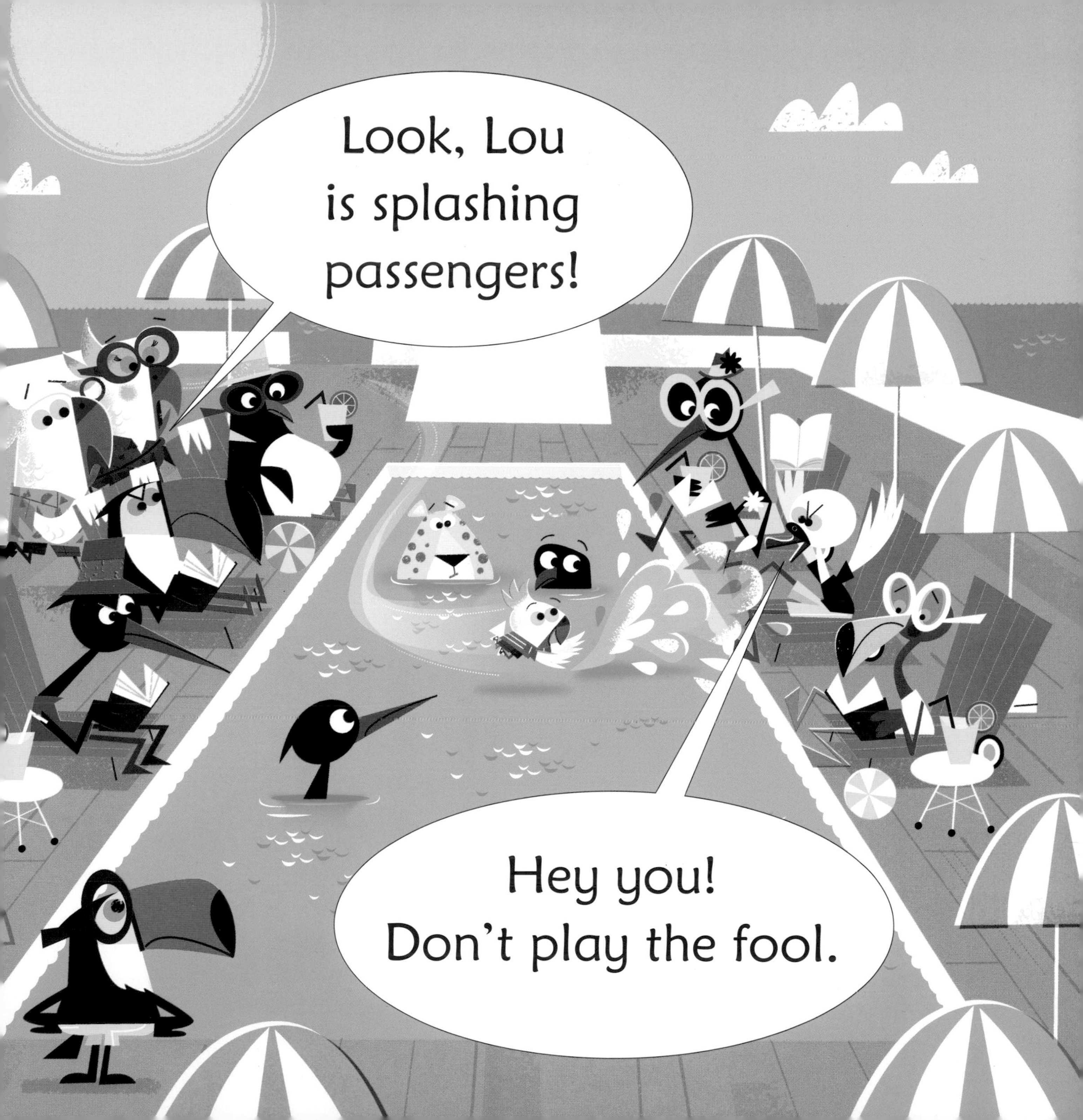
Look, Lou is splashing passengers!
Hey you! Don't play the fool.

They chase Lou to the lifeboats.

He seems to disappear.

But then he swoops out with a...

Boo!

Please stay away from here!

Some passengers are playing games with rings made out of rope.

Lou snatches three rings in his beak.

We'll bring them back – I hope!

On deck nine, in the dining room, they're serving cakes and tea.

Lou takes eight brownies off the plates
and gulps them down.

Yum-ee!

Lou veers into the theatre.

A show is underway.

He makes the dancers trip and slip.

The crowd shouts, "Go away!"

He flies above the ship's controls,
as Bruce and Sue appear.

Lou points down to the sea below
and gives the horn a blast.

"Look! Look!" he screams.

What has he seen?

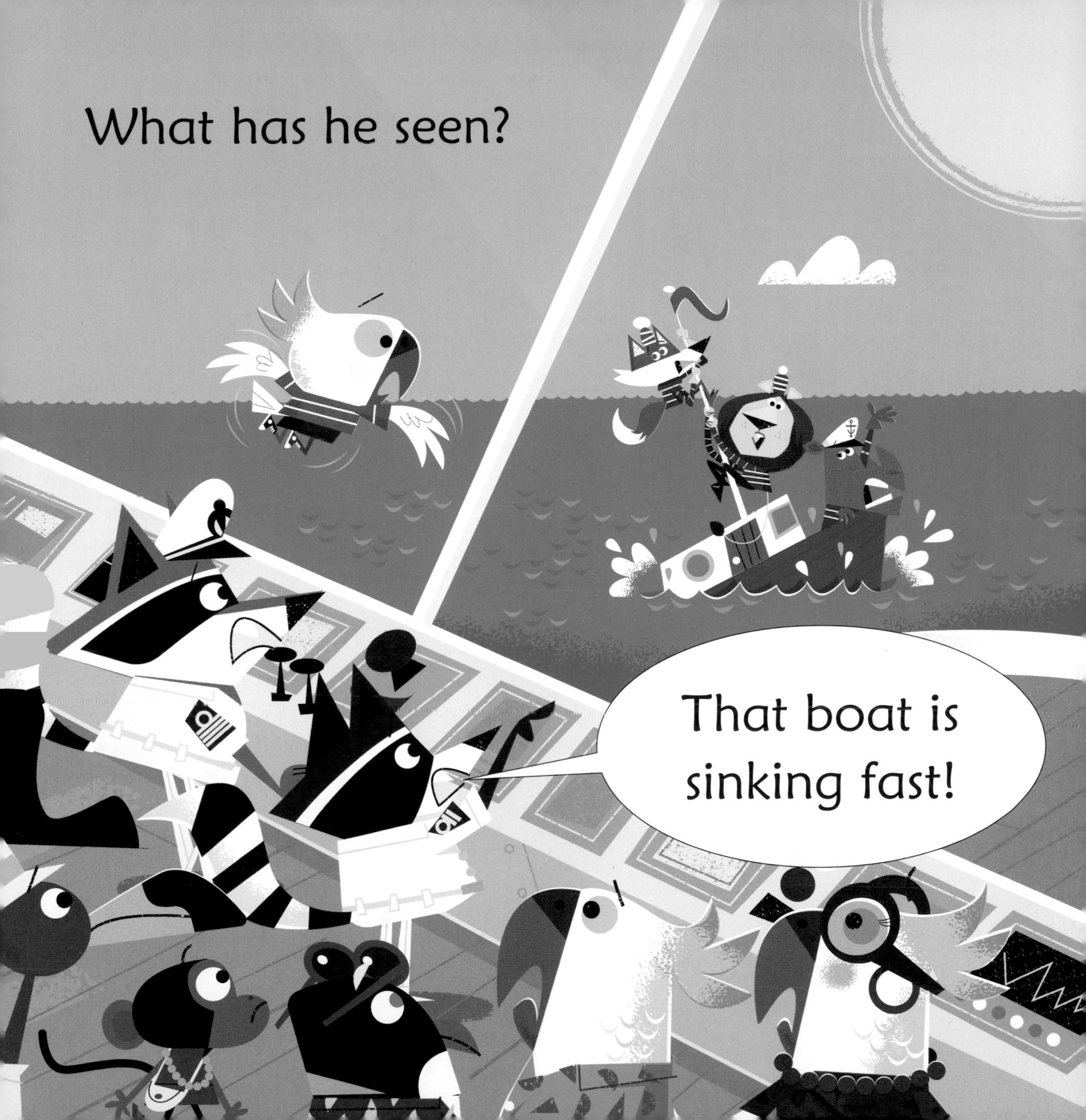

The small boat's crew is brought aboard.

Everyone gives Lou three cheers.

You clever cockatoo!

About phonics

Phonics is a method of teaching reading which is used extensively in today's schools. At its heart is an emphasis on identifying the *sounds* of letters, or combinations of letters, that are then put together to make words. These sounds are known as phonemes.

Starting to read

Learning to read is an important milestone for any child. The process can begin well before children start to learn letters and put them together to read words. The sooner children can discover books and enjoy stories and language, the better they will be prepared for reading themselves, first with the help of an adult and then independently.

You can find out more about phonics on the Usborne website at **usborne.com/Phonics**

Phonemic awareness

An important early stage in pre-reading and early reading is developing phonemic awareness: that is, listening out for the sounds within words. Rhymes, rhyming stories and alliteration are excellent ways of encouraging phonemic awareness.

In this story, your child will soon identify the *oo* sound, as in **cockatoo** and **cruise.** Look out, too, for rhymes such as **pool** – **fool** and **rope** – **hope.**

Hearing your child read

If your child is reading a story to you, don't rush to correct mistakes, but be ready to prompt or guide if needed. Above all, give plenty of praise and encouragement.

Edited by Lesley Sims
Designed by Hope Reynolds

Reading consultants: Alison Kelly and Anne Washtell

First published in 2022 by Usborne Publishing Ltd., Usborne House, 83-85 Saffron Hill,
London EC1N 8RT, England. usborne.com Copyright © 2022 Usborne Publishing Ltd. The name
Usborne and the Balloon logo are Trade Marks of Usborne Publishing Ltd.